THE GRAND ORIENT OF LOUISIANA

A SHORT HISTORY AND CATECHISM OF A LOST FRENCH RITE MASONIC BODY

INTRODUCTION BY MICHAEL R. POLL

A Cornerstone Book

The Grand Orient of Louisiana
A Short History and Catechism of a Lost
French Rite Masonic Body
Introduction by Michael R. Poll

A Cornerstone Book
Published by Cornerstone Book Publishers
Copyright © 2008 & 2024 by Cornerstone Book Publishers

Cornerstone Book Publishers
Hot Springs Village, AR

First Cornerstone Edition - 2008
Second Cornerstone Edition - 2024

www.cornerstonepublishers.com

ISBN: 978-1-934935-23-1

Introduction

Louisiana Masonry was born out of French Freemasonry. When the Grand Lodge of Louisiana was created in 1812, it was five French-speaking lodges that created it. The lodges were of a nature and worked the type of rituals that you would expect to find in France. By the 1830s, when most of the Grand Lodges in the United States had standardized their English-language rituals to be near mirror copies of each other, Louisiana lodges worked in several languages and rituals. The Grand Lodge created a *Chamber of Rites* to supervise its three official Masonic Rites: The York Rite (American-Webb ritual — as worked by most all other U.S. Jurisdictions), the Scottish Rite, and the French or Modern Rite. Louisiana was either out of step with the rest of U.S. Masonry or danced to a different tune — one similar to European Freemasonry. Not all of the Masons under the Grand Lodge were happy with this environment.

In the mid to late 1840s, dramatic events occurred in Louisiana due to English-speaking York Rite Masons and their desire for Louisiana to work in only one ritual, the York Rite ritual, like the rest of the U.S. Grand Lodges. After years of complaints, a second Grand Lodge was created alongside the Grand Lodge of Louisiana. Under pressure, and feeling that nothing else could be done, the Grand Lodge of Louisiana yielded and merged with this new body in 1850. Gone was the European nature of the Grand Lodge of Louisiana. Where there were once three Masonic Rites worked by the lodges, only the York Rite (American-Webb) was now authorized. The Scottish Rite and French or Modern Rite Masons, feeling tricked by the developments in the Grand Lodge, flew into rage at the turn of events. They felt something had to be done to correct this new situation.

The York lodges naturally aligned themselves with the Grand Lodge. Some Scottish Rite craft Masons, however, reached out to the Scottish Rite Supreme Council of Louisiana, with some passing under and remaining under its jurisdiction. Other Scottish Rite Masons, however, reached an agreement with the Grand Lodge, allowing them to continue to work in the Scottish Rite craft ritual. Today, due to this compromise, the 16th district of the Grand Lodge of Louisiana is composed of lodges working in the Scottish Rite craft ritual. But what about the French Rite lodges and Masons? What happened to them, and where did they go? It's not completely clear. The French Rite Masons had no superior body to seek relief from or pass under its jurisdiction. The French Rite became something of the *odd man out* in Louisiana Masonry.

The old *Chamber of Rites*, which accommodated and supervised the three rites working under the pre-1850 Grand Lodge of Louisiana, allowed lodges to work more than one of the three rites. Some Scottish Rite lodges, such as Etoile Polaire (Polar Star) #1 and Perseverance #4, were authorized to work in more than one of the rites. It would seem that the lodges (or, at least, the Masons) preferring the French or Modern Rite were somewhat absorbed by these Scottish Rite lodges. Both rites were French in nature, and they are far more similar in content and form than the York ritual. This absorption of the French Rite Masons occurred in the Scottish Rite lodges under the Grand Lodge and, also, the Supreme Council of Louisiana.

About 10 or 12 years ago, I was researching at Tulane University in New Orleans and found a very old small booklet in the George Longe Collection that was a Masonic catechism book for the French or Modern Rite. It was small, approximately 3 inches by 5 inches, with many unusually cut, irregularly shaped, and odd sized pages. Some pages were far larger, and some were cut so short that text was clearly missing. It carried the name of a body I was wholly unfamiliar with — *The Grand Orient of Louisiana*. Along with the incomplete ritual book was a short history that gave insight into the body, the reason for its creation, and more information on the post-1850 French Rite in Louisiana than had been previously available. Oddly enough, in reading the history, the author does not seem to be aware of the old Grand Lodge *Chamber of Rites* or the fact that the French or Modern Rite was worked by lodges in the pre-1850 Grand Lodge of Louisiana.

In addition to this find, I was able to locate in the same collection a Master Mason certificate (reproduced at the back of this present work) issued by a lodge under the jurisdiction of the Grand Orient of Louisiana. The certificate is significant for several reasons. According to the history included with the catechism, the Grand Orient of Louisiana was created and incorporated in 1879 by Masons affiliated with the Supreme Council of Louisiana who were dissatisfied with the practices of the Council. It can only be assumed that the Supreme Council provided a home for French Rite Masons following the Grand Lodge events of 1850 but might have given them less than expected freedom to work in the French or Modern Rite. An interesting point is that the Grand Orient of France might have lent some assistance in the creation of this new French Rite body. The history also tells us that this Grand Orient existed until about 1884 and then fell dormant. The undated preamble to the history suggests that a revival of this Grand Orient was being planned, but it is unclear as to the date of this reorganization or the length of time that it continued to exist after its reorganization. The Master Mason certificate is dated November 22, 1904, but it is uncertain how long before or after the date of this certificate that the body existed. The Mason receiving this certificate, René Métoyer, clearly did not remain forever under the jurisdiction of the Grand Orient of Louisiana. René Métoyer served as Sovereign Grand Commander of the Supreme Council of Louisiana in 1923 & 24 and again in 1926.

The early history of Louisiana Freemasonry is a rich yet very clouded story. Sadly, many aspects of our history are lost in the mists of inaccuracies due to lost documents, misreadings, assumptions, or jurisdictional squabbles resulting in skewed accounts. This little publication may be small and missing a few pieces, but it has opened a large historical and important door for researchers seeking a more comprehensive history of Freemasonry in Louisiana. The work will continue.

Michael R. Poll
New Orleans, LA
November, 2008

Progress
Grand Orient of Louisiana
(Modern Rite)

Organized on November 17, 1879
Incorporated on December 6, 1879.

(Ed. Note: The following was transcribed from the original document.)

This Masonic Power, which was founded in November, 1879, ceased functioning in December, 1884, after it had been decided that the lodges composing it were to lie dormant. Returned to activity by the revival of the R∴, L∴, the Crescent of Louisiana No. 1, it will soon be reorganized on a more extensive scale with the aid of the lodges which, in order to escape the tyranny of the Supreme Council of Louisiana, have submitted their request for Constitution on this jurisdiction.

An ardent appeal is hereby made to Masons of good faith to join a Body which, by its democratic constitution and by its spirit that is in closer harmony with the ideas of this century, faces a vast field of conquest for the cause which all of us cherish.

For the edification and instruction of all our brothers, we publish below an article reprinted from the "Official Bulletin" of the Grand Orient of Louisiana (June 15, 1880) which represents, so to say, the Declaration of Faith of the Institution.

These are principles which are valid at all times, and the facts mentioned, even if they took place some years ago, are still very appropriate to present circumstances.

Organization of the Grand Orient of Louisiana

On November 2, 7, and 17, 1879, following an unqualified abuse of power by the Supreme Council of Louisiana, a call was sent out to all the M .: M .: of the Orient.

In repudiating the autocratic despotism of the Sovereign Council of Louisiana, which was absolute and without appeal, it was under consideration to establish in New Orleans, with the purely moral help of the Grand Orient of France, a Rite which was absolutely legal and regular, as well as democratic, liberal and progressive.

A number of masons and several delegates of the Lodges answered our call; after stating the facts and reading a number of documents which were exhibited during this meeting, the following bases for the organization of the Grand Orient of Louisiana were accepted.

The undersigned M.: M.:, absolved only by their conscience and wishing to work for the progress and prosperity of Freemasonry, for the appeasement of the discord and the elimination of the schism separating and dividing the French Masonry (Grand Orient) and the American Masonry (Grand Lodges); wishing to repair, as far as it committed by this schism, to set straight the false situation of many betrayed Freemasons, and to arrive by reconciliation and by legal means at a union of these two

Masonic Powers, so that the motto "Liberty, Equality, Fraternity" may not be an empty word only; finally, with the purpose that the numerous American Masons, traveling in France, Italy, Belgium, Spain and Switzerland may find, in these different countries, the doors of all lodges wide open, and that the emigrants and European travelers, upon their arrival in this country, may find friendly hands, welcoming them as brothers;

Have enacted:

1.—That there shall be organized and established in New Orleans, for the State of Louisiana, a legal and regular Masonic Power which shall in no way be contrary and hostile to any Masonic Power which has already been legally established in this State; on the contrary, it shall do everything — absolutely everything — in order to enter into communication, union, correspondence and fraternal relations with such Powers.

2.—That this national and independent Masonic Power shall have the distinctive designation; "The Grand Orient of Louisiana."

3.—That this Power shall practice the Modern Rite (i.e. the reformed French Rite) which is not as yet practiced in the United States.

That, in consequence, practicing a new Rite, but one which has been universally recognized and differs from all the various Rites: the Scottish Rite, the York Rite, etc., which are practiced in this country, this new Rite shall not violate any of the "Landmarks", the supremacy, or the

Constitution of any Masonic Power already established in this State.

This legal point was fully recognized by the great and universal Masonic Convention which took place in Paris, in 1834, in which the following were represented: The Supreme Council of France, having its seat in Paris, the Supreme United Council of the Western Hemisphere, having its seat in New York, and the Supreme Council of the Empire of Brazil, having its east in Rio de Janeiro. The representatives of these three Supreme Councils, after having established that the Scottish Rite had for its purpose the study of philosophy, proclaimed and decreed in precise terms the following fundamental principles:

"The diversity of Rites entails necessarily a diversity of the Powers which direct them, as each Rite is absolutely independent of all the others; to recognize the independence of one Rite is to recognize the independence of all other Rites: this established a schism; this disturbs the entire Masonic order.

"The dogmatic or administrative action of the Power of a Rite can be legally exercised only over Masons of the same Rite who are subject to the jurisdiction of said Power;

"Each Masonic Power governs, under these General Statutes, only the Lodges of its Rite, situated within the limits of its territorial jurisdiction.

"The Power directing a Rite, within a recognized territorial jurisdiction, is absolutely sovereign and independent within the full extent of its territory." (Union Agreement, Edition of J.A. Boudon, Paris, 1836, page 12).

The Grand Orient of Louisiana shall strive for the physical, intellectual and moral progress of the individual: the political, religious and moral emancipation of the people; the abolition of slavery in places where it still exists; the extinction of poverty; the cooperation of the worker and the proletarian; and finally, shall strive for the solidarity of all men.

Therefore, the New Rite—to have any reason to exist —shall be occupied with all the political, religious and social questions representing progress and life, as well as the power and supremacy of every civilized nation. Otherwise, the outcome would be the same as with most of the old Rites: whose members were forbidden by their lords and masters, the Grand Commanders of these Rites, to consider these questions, thus stamping them as associations of benevolence and mutual assistance only; in eliminating these questions, there would be no point in organizing the New Rite.

And as far as religion is concerned, which must be fully independent of the State, this should be an entirely private matter between God and the human conscience. As, in studying the doctrines of all the religions which succeeded each other from the dawn of human association and which have been copied from one another, the philosopher, the sage, the man of good works must forcibly—if he is not a brute or a depraved person—arrive at the conclusion that an absolute tolerance is necessary in matters of religious belief. The Grand Orient shall have for its task to foster this idea among its members, each of whom shall be obliged to practice it. The true Free-masonry, our Freemasonry, which admits men of all religions, of all sects, which does not demand that anybody should swear on a certain gospel or on a certain code, but on his conscience and in order to approach more and more to absolute truth, our Freemasonry shall strive, in consideration of the problems of modern science and of the progress of our civilization, to learn and to teach others concerning the relations which might exist between the Creator and the Creature, between finite man and the infinite power that is God.

That is why the New Rite, while pardoning and excusing all beliefs and all weaknesses, assumes the task of stating and teaching the truth and of extirpating by reasoning, the errors and prejudices which have been brutally imposed during the infancy of mankind and against which, when man has arrived at the age where his spirit can no longer endure them (because of the high sum of intelligence evolved by humanity has outgrown them), he rises and revolts against himself, against all humanity and even against the Divine Force.

On the flag of the Grand Orient of Louisiana shall be inscribed only one device, a single word:

"Progrès!"

The Grand Orient of Louisiana will practice the Modern Rite, the Reformed French Rite.

This Rite comprises three degrees only:

1.—The Apprentice

2.—The Fellow Craft

3.—The Master Mason

Forming a harmonious whole which is complete and intelligent and in which all the degrees of all the other Rites have been included, but revised and corrected in order to arrive by a progressive work of elaboration at an absolute simplicity and at the practice of all good teachings of the true universal Masonry.

They shall embrace, above all, the study of man, principally as a material substance and comprising his relation with the exterior and material world which surrounds him; his relations to his family, his neighbors, his country. We shall learn about man's origins (Apprentice), what he is (Fellow Craft), and what his destiny is to be (Master). Then we shall study man in his immaterial aspect, trying to understand his relations (in his conscience) with God, the Great Architect of the Universe—the basis of his double nature (Master).

The organization of this Rite which, as stated above, will recognize only the first three degrees of Universal Freemasonry, the only ones not adverse to the dignity of free and intelligent man, shall be determined by a Constitution, copy of which shall be mailed, immediately after its publication, to all Masonic Bodies of the entire world.

Its official motto shall be:

Liberty! Equality! Solidarity!

All obligations imposed by the three words of this motto shall be scrupulously and rigorously fulfilled.

Racial equality will be practiced.

The Superior Body of the Grand Orient, destined to direct the Order and the Rite, shall be formed in a democratic manner by means of delegations, by the votes of all the lodges which shall constitute it and which shall form part of it (3 members of each lodge, independently of all the lodges which this Body, thus composed, shall consider eligible to join).

The official language shall be French. However, all notifications and communications addressed to different foreign Orients can be made in the language of said Orients.

The lodges under the jurisdiction of this Grand Orient shall in their work use the language of their choosing, but all their communications and reports made to the Grand Orient shall be made in French.

With the exception of the clauses of the oath of allegiance, required in writing of all their officers and members, and with the exception of the restrictions imposed by the Articles of the Incorporation Act concerning them, the member lodges shall be absolutely free and independent; nothing shall at any time be imposed on them without their free will and consent, as the rulers of the Order shall consist of delegates chosen by said lodges among their members.

The number of the delegates of the lodges of the Grand Orient entrusted to compose this Body shall never be less than three members of each lodge. These delegates shall be chosen and elected by secret a ballot during the last December meeting of each lodge.

They shall take possession and shall be installed at the Grand Orient by the Grand Master or by the member entrusted with this task during the first January meeting, and the election by secret ballot of all the Officers of this Body, to hold office for one year only, shall take place at the following meeting of the Grand Orient.

All Officers of the Grand Orient can be reelected.

All the founding members of the Grand Orient shall, however, after they have been replaced in their functions, remain active members of said Grand Orient, provided they are active members of a lodge under the jurisdiction of said Grand Orient.

Finally, a Special Committee shall be named in order to prepare and present for adoption of a General Meeting, which shall be convoked as an extraordinary meeting on November 17, 1879:

1. —A constitution and Regulations based on those of the Grand Orients of France, Italy, Spain, and Belgium, amended in the spirit of liberty and progress;
2. —An Act of Incorporation of said order in the State of Louisiana;

3. —A notification of appeal addressed to all the Regular Orders of all the Rites, distributed all over the world, in order to ask for the recognition of our Order as a legal and regular Power and to enter with them into communication and fraternal relations.
4. —A proclamation appealing to all Masons, active or dormant, to lend their hands to our work.

The present agreements were definitely accepted, signed and put into execution, and the Grand Orient of Louisiana—Modern Rite—was organized on November 17, 1879.

THE GRAND ORIENT OF LOUISIANA

CATECHISM

INSTRUCTION

OF THE

FIRST DEGREE

Apprentice

What is the tie that unites us?
Freemasonry.

What is Freemasonry?
Freemasonary is an institution purely philosophical, which has object, the physical, Intellectual, and moral progress of the individual; as well as the political, religious and social emancipation of nations

Are you a Fredmason?
My Bros .˙. reconize me as such.

To what Rite do you belong?
To the modern R. F. and eccepted.

What do you understand by Rite?
One of the different forms of Freemasonry

What is your object in attending Lodge?
I come to learn my duties and my rights as a man, as a free citizen and as a Freemason

Where were you received a Free mason?

I. in a Lodge just and perfect.

What is the requisites for Lodges to be just and perfect?

Three govern her, five give her light, and Seven renders her just and perfect

Who are the three?

The W.∴ M.∴ and the two wardens

Who are the five?

The W.∴ M.∴, the Wardens.∴ the Orat.∴ and the Secretary, who are the five lights of all the Lodges just and perfect.

Who are the seven?

The five first off ',, and two active members of the L.∴

Is not a Lodge designated under another title?

It also bears the name of Ateller or work shop,

Why?

Because a masonic Lodge is but an assembly of workmen who all work for the progress and happiness of humanity; some with their intelligence and others with the physical powers with which the Grand Architect of the Universe has endowed them.

How long have you been a Free. mason?

Since the day that I receive light.

How will I know that you are a Freemason?

By my signs, words, and touchings

How are the signs made?

By Squars, Levels, and Perpendicular.

Give me the sign.

(He give it.)

What is the signification of this sign

I would rather have my throat cut,

than to become a traitor to the cause of Freemasonry. and fail to the promises that I have solemnly made in presence of my Bros .˙.

Give the touching to Brother expert
He give it to the expert who after receiving it says, the touching is perfectly correct.

Give me the sacred word.
W.˙. M.˙. I know neither how to read nor write my knowledge is limited to spelling, give me the first letter and I will give you the second.

Give me yourself the first letter.
In this manner the sacred word is spelt

What does this word signify?
Power

Why do Freemasons have the number THREE in their batteries, acclamations and manner of working?

Because the number THREE is the representation of the Infinite, which is God, and of the Finite which is man, and that God as in man there is Power, Wisdom and Beauty.

What is the form of our lodge?

A rectangle parallelogram.

In what direction is the length?

From the East to the West.

Its Width?

From centre to septentrion.

Its height?

From Zenith to Nadir, that is to say, from the surface of the earth to the infinite.

What is the meaning of these dimentions?

That masonry is universal, and that it should be accessible to all men, without regard to their ccuntry.

Why is the lodge situated from East to West?

Because Freemasonry like the first rays of the sun came to us from the East.

What do you understand by the word lodge?

We call lodge, the secret place where Freemasons shelter themselves to cover their labors.

Why do Freemasons assemble in a secret place?

In order not to be disturbed in their labors by the enemies of Fraternity, Equality and Liberty, and to accomplish more surely the great work of Freemasonary.

What sustains our Lodge?

Three large pillers, named Wisdom Power, and Beauty, which are symbolized by the W∴ M∴ and the Two wardens

How were you introduce in the Lodge on the day of your initiation

By ✳✳✳ hard knocks.

What do these knocks mean?

Ask and you will be opened.

Have you received what you were asking ?

I received the masonic light, which I asked; that is to say, the philosophical doctrines that are to guide me in the pro, ∴ world and insure my happinness there if followed were devulged to me.

Have you found what you were searching

I found have a society of Free men, who became my Bros . ∴ and who have promised me assistance and protection when needed.

When you knock did we open ?
You open the doors of the Temple, where is hidden the masons secret which is the duty of all Apprentice masons to deserve

How were you disposed of, after your introduction in this Temple?
I was submitted to several physical and morals trails and having sustainedl

them to the satisfaction of the brethren present, I was constituted Apren.˙. Mason.

Where is the place of apprentice in' Lodge ?
The North. which symbolizes the point the less lightened' for the apprentices have only received a beginning of instruction in masonary.
What is your age as apprentice mason ?

✳✳✳ years W.˙. M.˙.
What is the wages of an app.˙. mason?
Fourty three cents.

INSTRUCTION

OF THE

FELLOW CRAFT

DEGREE,

A. The letter G. is known to me.

Q. What is the signification of that letter?

A, It signifies Geometry and God.

Q. Why did you receive the degree of Fellow-craft?

A. In order to work to the best of my strength and ability with all Free Masons, my companions and brethren, to the final triumph of Masonic principles.

Q. What is the great work contem; plated by Free Masons?

A. To make all men equal by labor, as a perfect equality will never reign in this world unless the principles of true Free Masonry are known and put in practice.

Q. How were you received Fellow-craft?

A. With my eyes wide open and in

Q. What did you see on entering the lodge?

A. Two large columns, one at the left hand with the letter B. and the other one at the right hand with the letter J.

Q. What was their composition?
A. Molten or cast brass.

Q. What was their dimensions ?
A. Eighteen cubits in heighth, twelve in circumference and four in diameter.

Q. Why were they cast hollow?
A. To better preserve the tools and archives of Free Masonry and also the money destined to the payment of fellow craft and apprentices.

Q. How did you gain admission?
A. By a sign, by a pass word, by a sacred word and by a grip.

Q. Give me the sign?

Q. What does it denote?

A. That I would rather have my heart torn out by the roots than to violate the promises I made in the presence of my brothers assembled in this lodge.

Q. Give the pass-word to Brother Exp.

(Pass'word is given.)

Q. Give the sacred word to brother Exp.

(The sacred word is given.)

Q. Give the grip to brother, Exp.

(The grip is given.)

Q. How were you disposed of after you entered the Lodge?

A, I made five voyages, In the first I had in my hand a mallet and a chisel; in the second a ruler and a pair of compasses; in the third a ruler and a lever; in the fourth a ruler and a square.

A. The mallet and chisel serve to pare and hew the rough stone in taking off its asperity and giving it its proper form; the ruler and compass are tools by which lines are drawn on plain and smooth surfaces; the lever is destined to raise heavy bodies, and the square to form equal sides and right angles.

Q What is the moral and symbolical meaning of these tools?

A. By the mallet and chisel we mean that a true Free Mason ought to divest himself of his prejudices and be governed and measured by the eternal principles of morality; by the compasses that we ought to su tan ourselves in truth and justice; by the lever, that it is our duty to oppose a determined resistance to all that is

actions by the opinions of good men, our lives by the precepts of philosophers.

Q. How did you make the five voyages?

A. With my hands entirely free.

Q. Why?

A. As an indication to the fellow-craft that it is only after long and tedious labor that he will be permitted to rest and enjoy his freedom and independence.

Q. Has our lodge any ornament?

A. It has, first the Mosaic or chequered Pavement, represeating this world, which, though checkered over with good and evil, brethren may work together thereon and not stumble; second, the Blazing Star; as a symbol of the true light which Free

third, the Cord of Union which surrounds our lodge, teaching all Free Masons to live together as a family of brethren, in order to better defend all their political, religious, civil and social rights;

Q. Has your lodge any Jewels?

A. It has three, movable and immovable.

Q, What are the movable Jewels?

A. The Level, Plumb and Trowel,

Q. What do they teach?

A. The Level equality the Plumb rectitude of life and conduct and the Trowel teaching all Free Masons that they ought not only to forgive thetr mutual wrongs and offenses, but also to cement and strenghthen the ties of Brotherhood.

Q. What are the three immovable Jewels?

Q. What do they represent?

A. The Rough Ashlar represents man in his rude and imperfect state of nature: the Perfect Ashlar represents man in that state of perfection to which all hope to arrive by means of a virtuous life and education, and the Tresle Board is the emblem of reffection and wisdom.

Q. Where do the Fellcw'craft i in the temple ?

A. In the South or in the North.

Q. Why in the South?

A, To help M. M, in their work and to profit by their lessons

Q. Why in the North?

A. To assist the Apprentices in their works.

Q. How do the Fellow-craft work

Q. What is your age as a Fellow craft?

A. *** ** years.

Q. What is the wages of a Fellow-craft?

A. Forty;five cents (or Shekels.)

INSTRUCTION

~OF THE~

MASTER MASON

DEGREE,

Q. Are you a M. M.?

A. The Acacia is known to me.

Q. What does Acacia symbolize?

A. Immortality.

Q. Where were you initiated to the degree of **M. M** ?

A In the Sanctum Sanctorum f Holy of Holies;

Q. What did you see on entering ?

A. Mourning and consternation in remembrance of a sad and calamitous event,

Q. What was that event?

A. The death of Hiram Abi, who had been murdered by three companions.

Q. Is that murder a real and true fact?

A. It is viewed by Free Masons as a legend.

Q. What is the meaning of such a fiction ?

A. Hiram Abi represents justice and truth, and the three companions ignorance, hypocrisy and ambition.

Q. How were you then disposed of?

A. A brother took me by a coffin and requested me to say whether I had participated in the death of the pesson there lying. I answered no.

Q. What was the meaning of such a question and of the sight offered to your eyes ?

A. To impress on my mind that no man has the right to make an attempt npon the life ot his fellow beings, and that, in the third degree, mysteries of dcath should be fully illustrated and explained.

Q. What next was made to you ?

A. I had to make three voyages,

A. What is the philosophical or symbolical meaning of these three voyages?

A. That there are three distinct pe

riods in human life Youth, Manhood
and Senility. Durihg the first period
we are all apprentices and know very
little; during the second, man be-
comes the companion of all reasonable
beings made by the Grand Architect
of the Unlverse, after His own image;
and finally, during the third, man is
the great master of life, since he
knows all its sufferings and pleasures,
and, being taught by experleuce, he
fully understands the necessity of and
raasons for death,

Q. Where were you disposed of
after these three voyages?

A. I was requested to take the
solemn obligation of the M, M.

Q. Can yon give me a proof that
you remember your promise?

A. I can by giving you the sign of
the third degree.

Q. Give it.

(He gives the sign.)

Q. what does it mean?

A, That I would rather have my body severed in two than to violate the promise made; not only to keep silent about all secrets of the third degree, but also never to harm or injure the wife; daughter, sister or mother of a brother.

Q. Do you know another sign?

A. I do.

Q, what is it ?

A. The sign of horror which was made when the pall thrown over the corps of Hir Abi was taken away.

Q. Make it.

(The sign is made,)

Q, What is the Pass word of the Third Degree?

(The pass—word is given.)

Q. What is the sacred word?

A. I am ready to give it in a prop

way. I have first to give the five points of perfection,

Q. What are the five points of perfection?

A. Hand to hand to show that we are united as two brothers; foot to foot indicates that whatever may be the distance separating the two free–m, they are bound to run to the assistance of each other; knee to knee to remind us that we have common creed ; the belief in a Grand Architect of the Universe, and, further should we kneel before God, we never kneel as Free M, in presence of any man; breast to breast, that we ought to bury in our bosoms all secrets instrusted to us by a brother; left hand on right shoulder, that it is our duty never to permit a brother to be slandered when absent, that on the contrary we ought to defend and protect his reputation.

Q. What is your age as M. M, ?

A. *** *** *** years and more ; ....years because that number is required to have a just and perfect Lodge, and more, beeause I am now familiar with all secrets and mysteries of this modernrite of Free Masonry.

Q. Should your life be in great danger, what would you do?

A. I will give the sign of distress.

Q. Give it.   (The sign of distress is given with the words--to me the **w,** wd-s.

Q· What was the dimension of **the** grave of Hiram?

A.. Three feet in width, five feet **in** depth and seven feet in length.

Q, What are the wages of a **M, M.**

A. Forty-seven shekels.

Master Mason Certificate of René Métoyer

Next Page

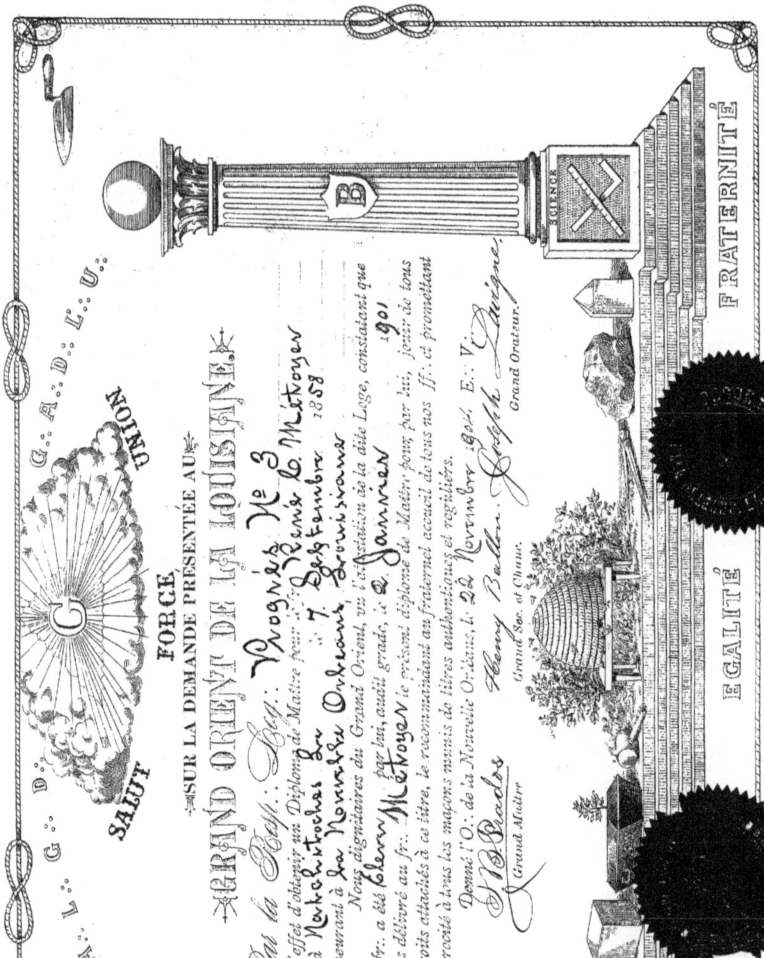

Opposite page:

Master Mason Certificate dated November 22, 1904 for René Métoyer issued by Progrés Lodge No. 3 under the Grand Orient of Louisiana.

René Métoyer would later move to the jurisdiction of the Supreme Council of Louisiana and serve as its Sovereign Grand Commander in 1923, 24 and 1926.

Living Freemasonry
A Better Path to Travel
by Michael R. Poll
6x9 Softcover & Hardcover 180 pages
6x9 Softcover Large Print Edition 201 pages
ISBN 978-1-93493-595-8
ISBN (Hardcover) 978-1-61342-424-7
ISBN (Large Print) 979-8-88468-301-3

The Particular Nature of Freemasons
by Michael R. Poll
6x9 Softcover & Hardcover 158 pages
6x9 Softcover Large Print Edition 211 pages
ISBN 978-1-61342-346-2
ISBN (Hardcover) 978-1-61342-903-7
ISBN (Large Print) 979-8-32153-619-3

The Scottish Rite Papers
A Study of the Troubled History of the Louisiana and
US Scottish Rite in the Early to Mid-1800s
by Michael R. Poll
6x9 Softcover & Hardcover 275 pages
ISBN 978-1-61342-345-5
ISBN (Hardcover) 978-1-61342-404-9

Historical Inquiry into the Origins
of the Ancient and Accepted Scottish Rite
by James Foulhouze
Edited by Jonathan K. Poll
Foreword by Michael R. Poll
6x9 Softcover & Hardcover 288 pages
ISBN: 978-1-61342-026-3
ISBN (Hardcover) 978-1-61342-405-6

Seeking Light
The Esoteric Heart of Freemasonry
by Michael R. Poll
6x9 Softcover & Hardcover 156 pages
ISBN 978-1-61342-257-1
ISBN (Hardcover) 978-1-61342-438-4

Measured Expectations
The Challenges of Today's Freemasonry
by Michael R. Poll
6x9 Softcover & Hardcover 178 pages
6x9 Softcover Large Print Edition 210 pages
ISBN 978-1-61342-294-6
ISBN (Hardcover) 978-1-61342-410-0
ISBN (Large Print) 979-8-88457-534-9

A Masonic Evolution
The New World of Freemasonry
by Michael R. Poll
6x9 Softcover & Hardcover 160 pages
6x9 Softcover Large Print Edition 196 pages
ISBN 978-1-61342-315-8
ISBN (Hardcover) 978-1-61342-407-0
ISBN (Large Print) 979-8-32161-632-1

**The Ancient and Accepted Scottish Rite
in Thirty-Three Degrees**
by Robert B. Folger
Introduction by Michael R. Poll
6x9 Softcover 2 Volumes 822 pages
ISBN (Vol. 1) 978-1-61342-240-3
ISBN (Vol. 2) 978-1-61342-241-0

An Encyclopedia of Freemasonry
by Albert Mackey
Revised by William J. Hughan and Edward L. Hawkins
Foreword by Michael R. Poll
8.5 x 11 Softcover 2 Volumes 960 pages
ISBN (Vol. 1) 978-1-61342-252-6
ISBN (Vol. 2) 978-1-61342-253-3

Masonic Enlightenment
The Philosophy, History and Wisdom of Freemasonry
Edited by Michael R. Poll
6x9 Softcover & Hardcover 240 pages
ISBN 978-1-61342-237-3
ISBN (Hardcover) 978-1-61342-426-1

The Freemasons Key
A Study of Masonic Symbolism
Edited by Michael R. Poll
6x9 Softcover & Hardcover 264 pages
ISBN 978-1-61342-228-1
ISBN (Hardcover) 978-1-61342-423-0

Our Stations and Places
Masonic Officer's Handbook
by Henry G. Meacham
Revised by Michael R. Poll
6x9 Softcover & Hardcover 178 pages
ISBN 978-1-61342-331-8
ISBN (Hardcover) 978-1-61342-697-5

In His Own (w)Rite
by Michael R. Poll
6x9 Softcover & Hardcover 180 pages
ISBN 978-1-61342-157-4
ISBN (Hardcover) 978-1-61342-437-7

Knights & Freemasons
The Birth of Modern Freemasonry
By Albert Pike & Albert Mackey
Edited by Michael R. Poll
Foreword by S. Brent Morris
6x9 Softcover & Hardcover 176 pages
ISBN 978-1-61342-150-5
ISBN (Hardcover) 978-1-61342-408-7

10,000 Famous Freemasons
4 Vol. Softcover Edition
by William Denslow
Foreword by Harry S. Truman
Cornerstone Foreword by Michael R. Poll
6x9, Softcover 4 Volumes 1,515 pages
ISBN Vol. 1: 1887560319
ISBN Vol. 2: 1887560793
ISBN Vol. 3: 1887560424
ISBN Vol. 4: 1887560068

Robert's Rules of Order: Masonic Edition
Revised by Michael R. Poll
6x9 Softcover & Hardcover 212 pages
ISBN 978-1-61342-231-1
ISBN (Hardcover) 978-1-61342-914-3

Masonic Words and Phrases
Edited by Michael R. Poll
6x9 Softcover & Hardcover 134 pages
ISBN 978-1-61342-167-3
ISBN (Hardcover) 978-1-61342-439-1

Cornerstone Book Publishers
www.cornerstonepublishers.com

New Orleans Scottish Rite College
http://www.no-sr-college.com

Clear, Easy to Watch
Scottish Rite and Craft Lodge
Podcast & Video Education

Thank you for buying this Cornerstone book!

For over 25 years now, I've tried to provide the Masonic community with quality books on Masonic education, philosophy, and general interest. Your support means everything to us and keeps us afloat. Cornerstone is by no means a large company. We are a small family-owned operation that depends on your support.

Please visit our website and have a look at the many books we offer as well as the different categories of books.

If your lodge, Grand Lodge, research lodge, book club, or other body would like to have quality Cornerstone books to sell or distribute, write us. We can give you outstanding books, prices, and service.

Thanks again!
Michael R. Poll
Publisher

Cornerstone Book Publishers
1cornerstonebooks@gmail.com
http://cornerstonepublishers.com

www.ingramcontent.com/pod-product-compliance
Lightning Source LLC
Chambersburg PA
CBHW031140270326
41931CB00007B/634